I0471832

Cultural Arts in Columbus Book Series Vol 3
Murals and Street Arts in Columbus Ohio
Part 2 Arts in Franklinton
Shoichiro Nakamura

Printed by CreateSpace, Sold at Amazon.com
Published in 2018
ISBN-13: 978-1546935636

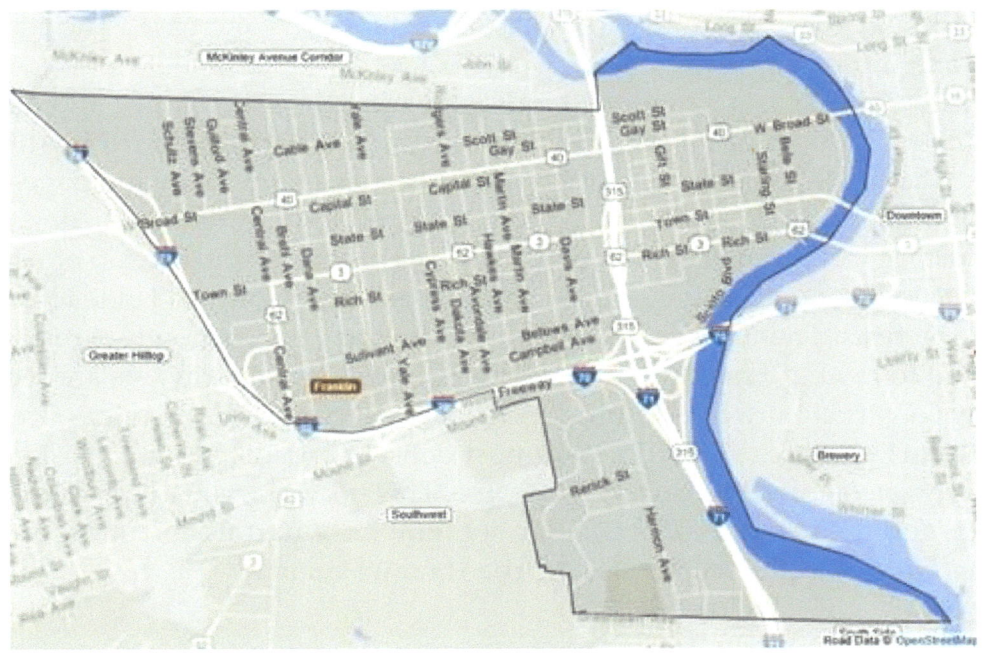

Brief History of Franklinton Columbus OH

Franklinton is an area adjacent to downtown of city of Columbus, as shown in map on the previous page west and south of Scioto river, nearly north of I70 and east of the Hilltop area. Franklinton peninsula is the east side of Franklinton between Rt315 and Scioto River, where Scioto river is turning a half circle. Median house hold income is about $19K, and the house hold income of 37% of population is less than 10K. It is reported that 59% of the households in the area have no person of a college degree.

However, Franklinton played a very important role in the development of Columbus. In late 18th century, the early pioneers who came to Columbus area preferred to settle in Franklinton, because this area had most fertile soil for farming, and connection to Ohio River through Scioto River. By the middle of the 19th century, population and industry increased and four railways were built in Franklinton.

However, Franklinton was plagued by flooding. During the 19th century, there were 12 time of minor flooding in Franklinton. Then, the severest flooding occurred in1913, which killed 93 people and destroyed 500 houses and every bridge. The photos on following pages show the landscapes of flooding in 1913. Another flooding occurred in 1959 again, when.

In 1983, the city of Columbus issued an ordinance to prohibit construction of new buildings. In 2004, Franklinton Floodwall was completed, which is 7 miles long and able to protect the area from up to 31 feet crests. Then, the ordinance of prohibiting construction was released. City of Columbus started to rebuild Franklinton as another Short North. Today, we are seeing remarkable new construction works in progress in the east part of Franklinton.

Regarding the art activities, Franklinton is most densely populated with artist's studios, although they are not visible yet to ordinary people. This book starts with photographs of the flooding in 1913, and the rest is a collection of photographs of murals and street arts in Franklinton art district and the scenes of the Urban Scrawl auction.

Lucus Sullivant had the most important role in the earliest settlement in Columbus, which started in Franklinton.

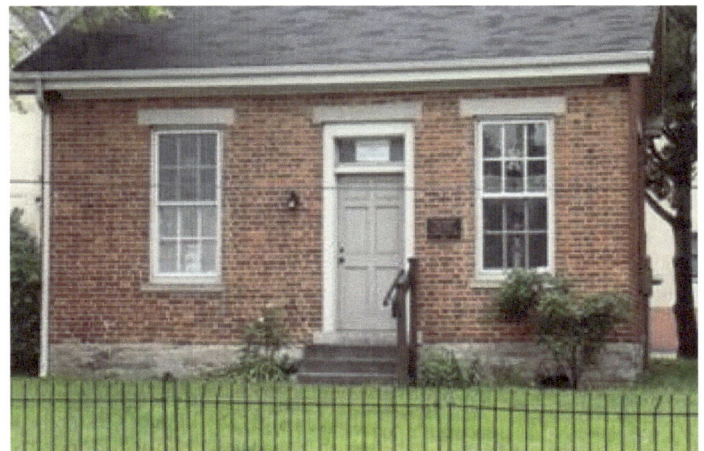
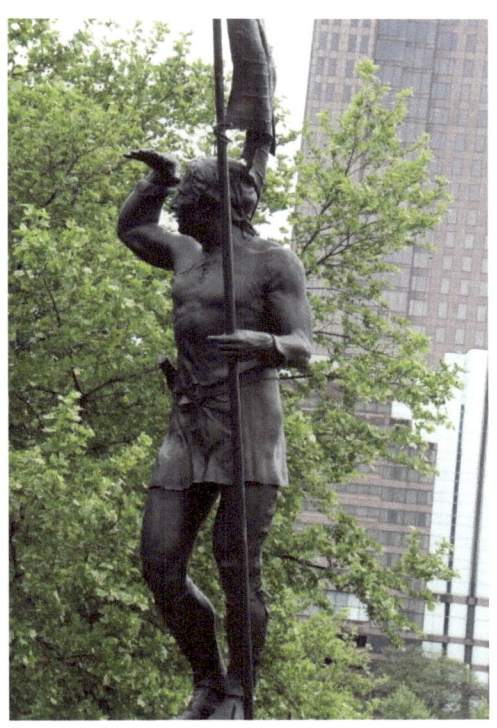
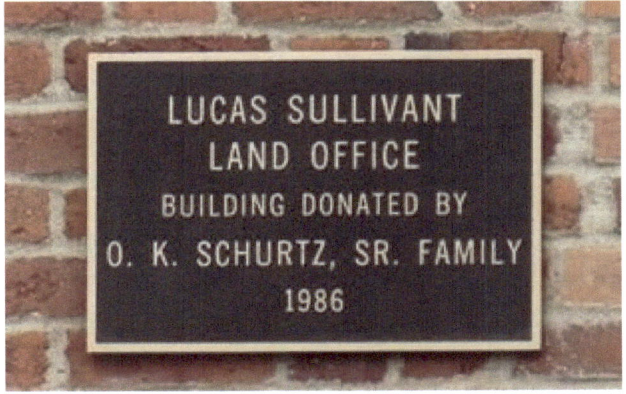

1913 Flooding in Franklinton

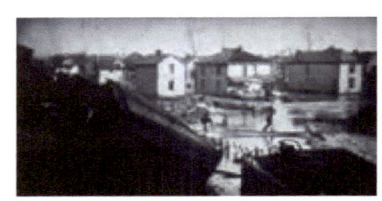
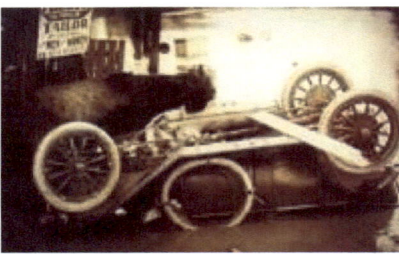
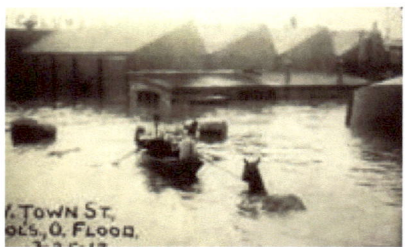

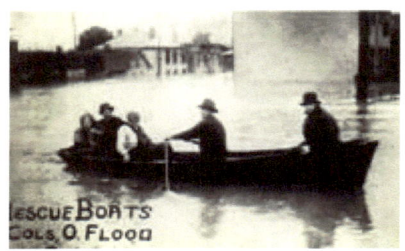
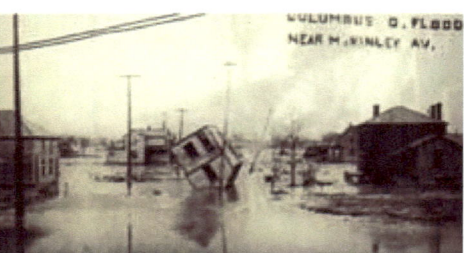

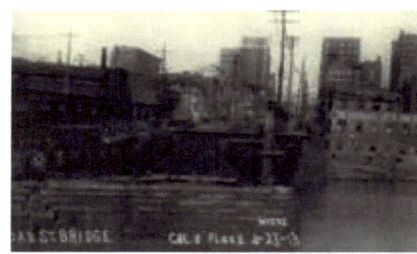
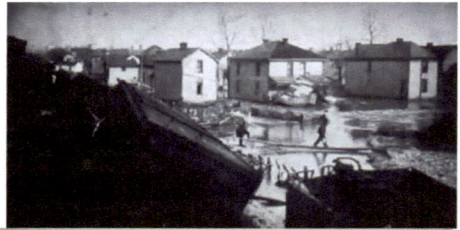

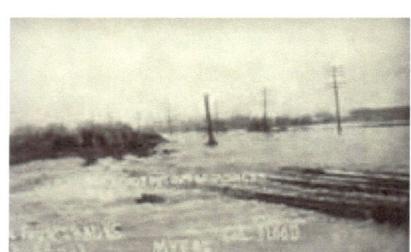
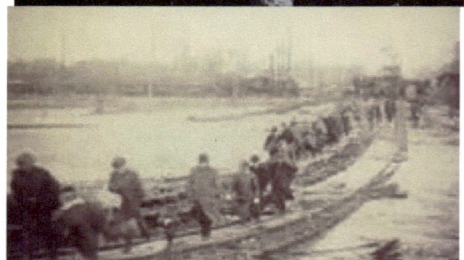

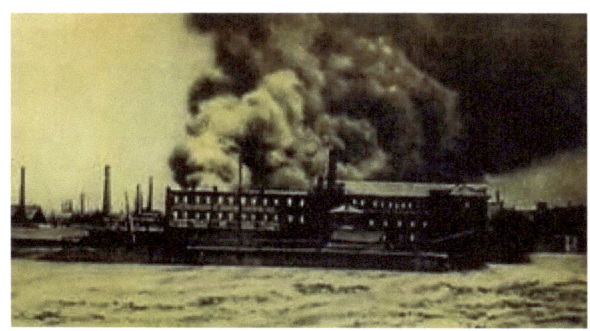

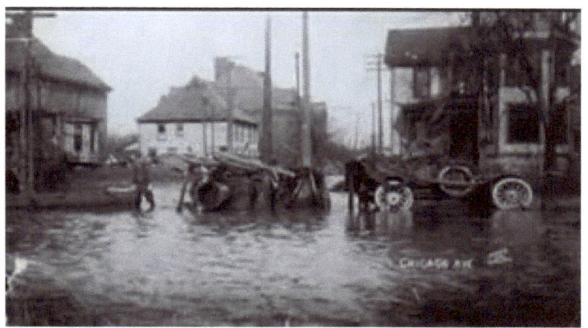

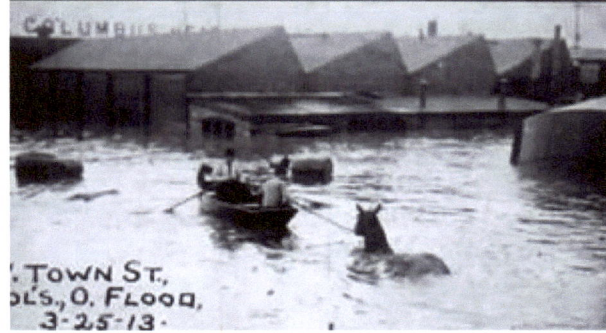

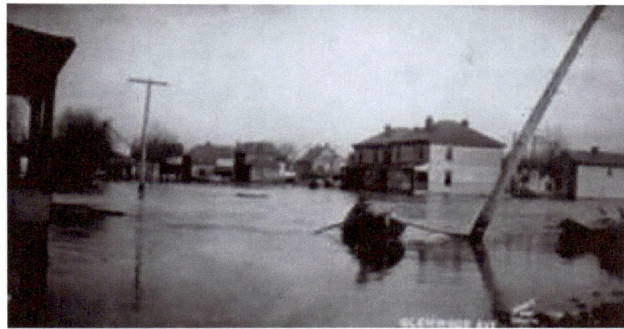

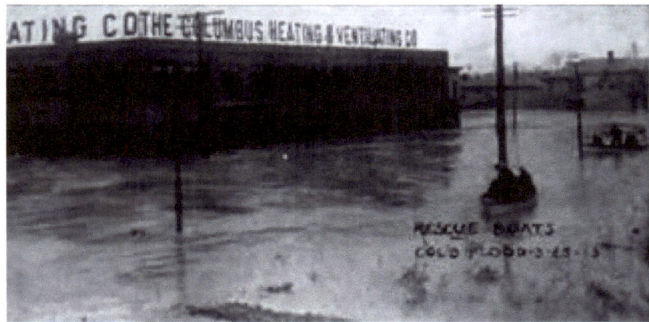

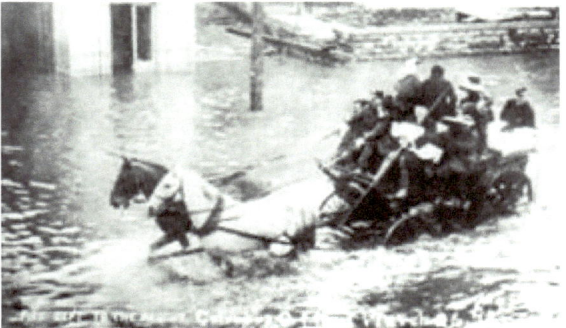

A Sculpture of American Bison at Souder Ave and W Broad Street

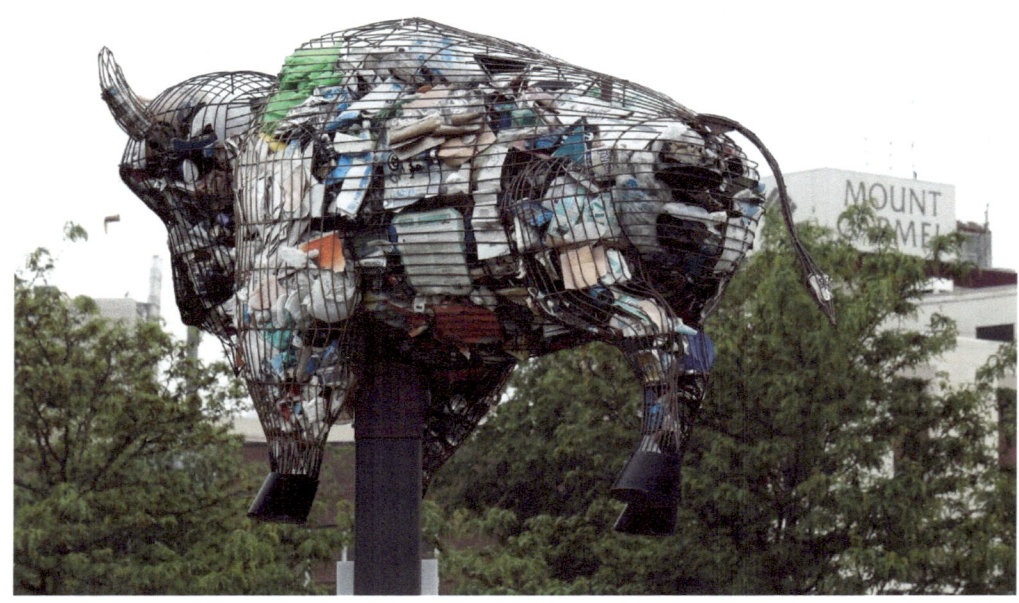

This sculpture implicates at least two things. First is that this land was once roamed by American bisons. In fact, when Lucus Sullivant arrived in his first travel from Kentucky, he chose to pass through American bison's trails. Second, by stuffing the sculpture by trashes, efforts of cleaning up Franklinton area by removing trashes is called for.

Tiny murals near Souder Ave and W Broad St by school kids

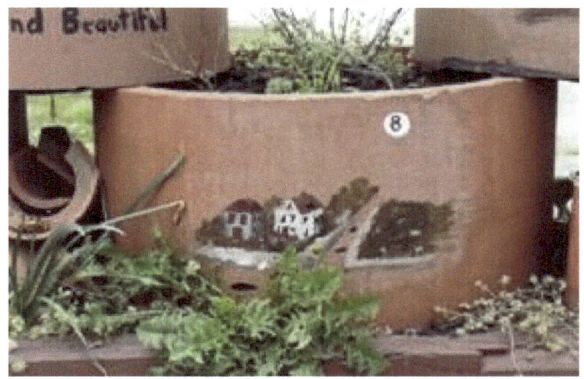

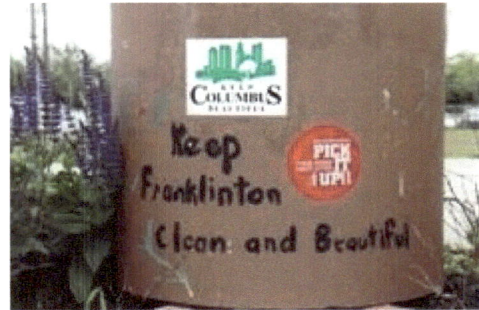

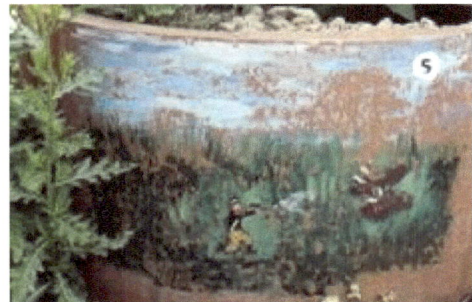

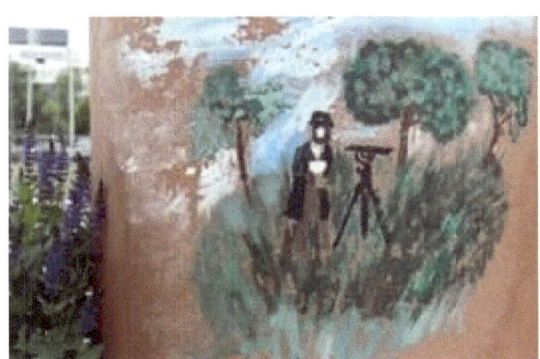

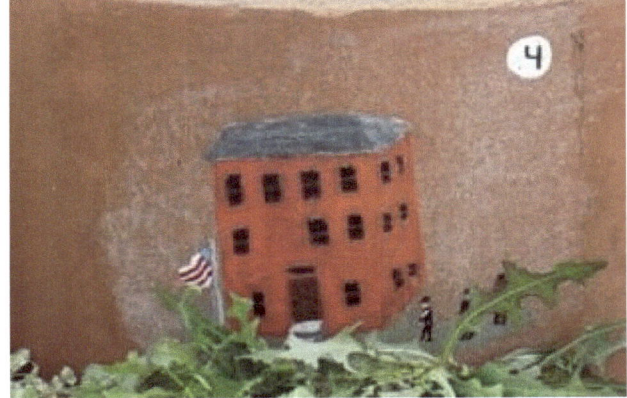

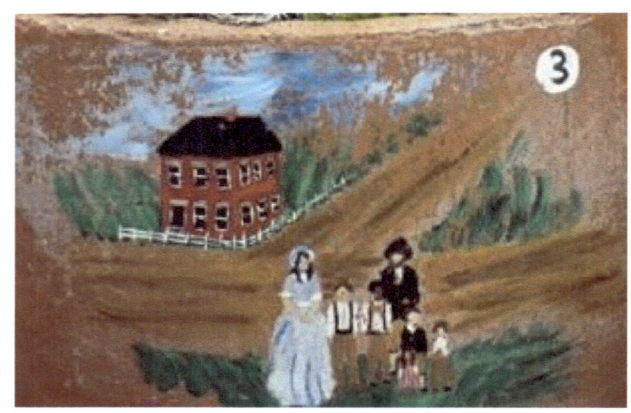
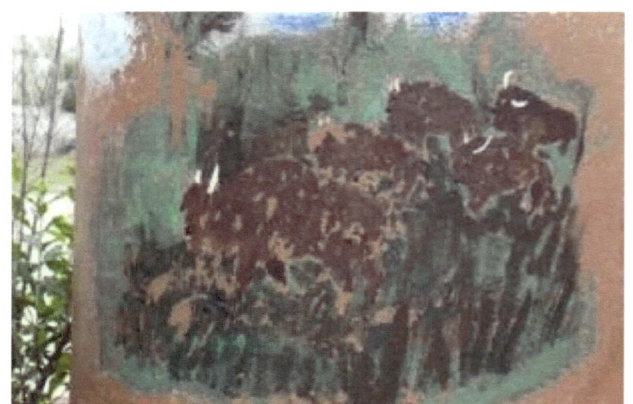
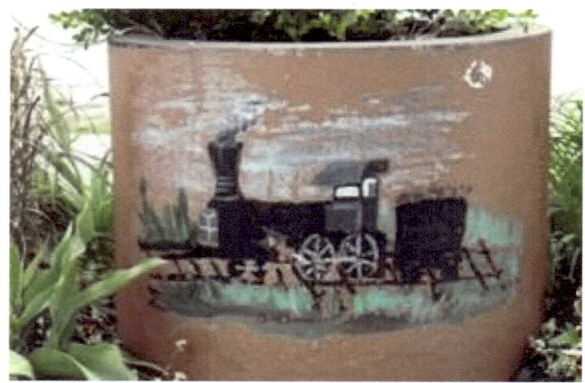
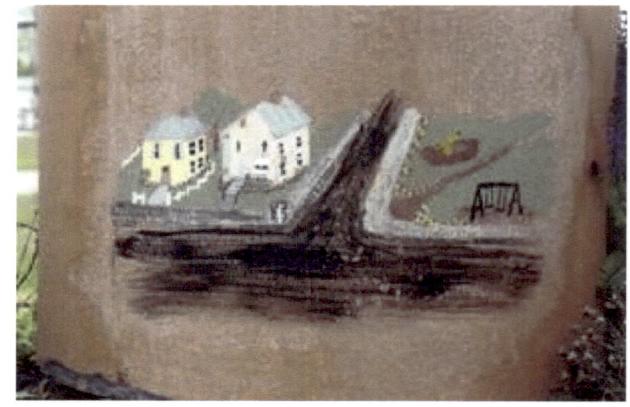

Murals along W Broad St

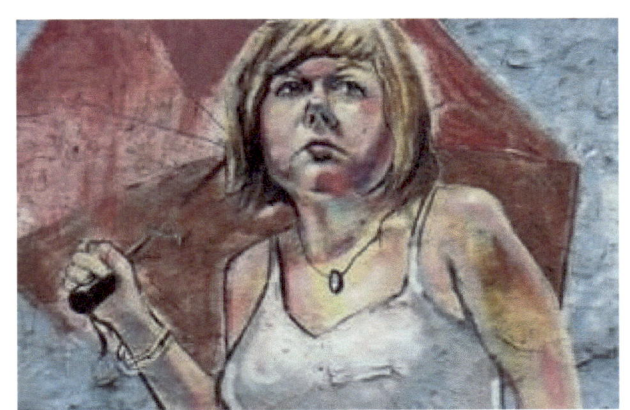 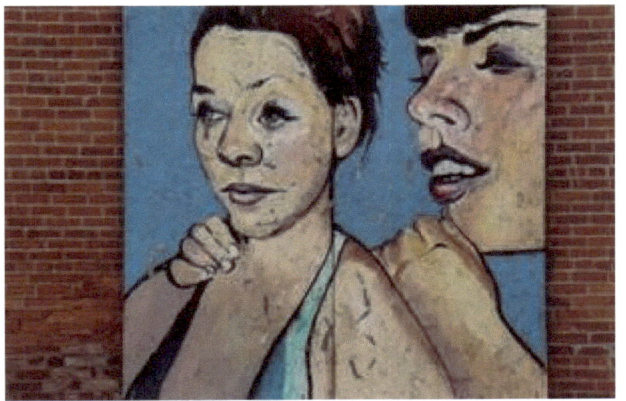

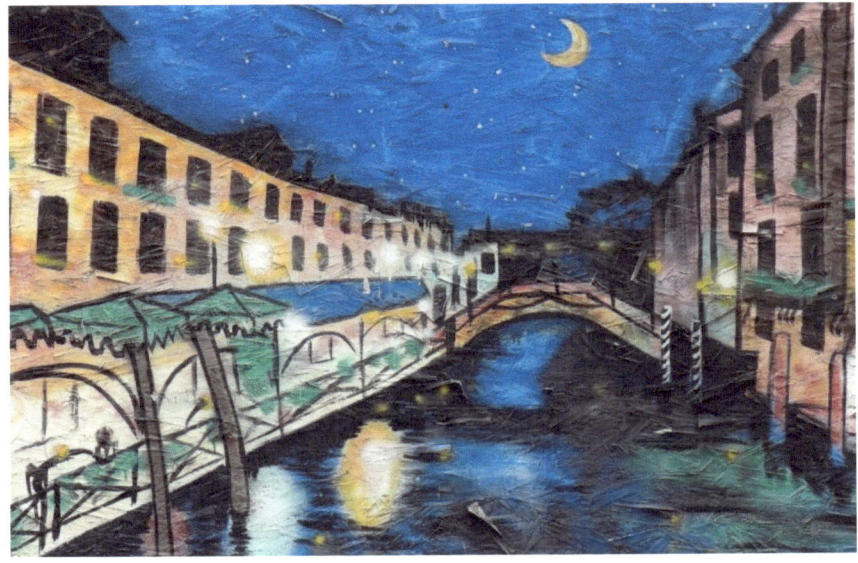

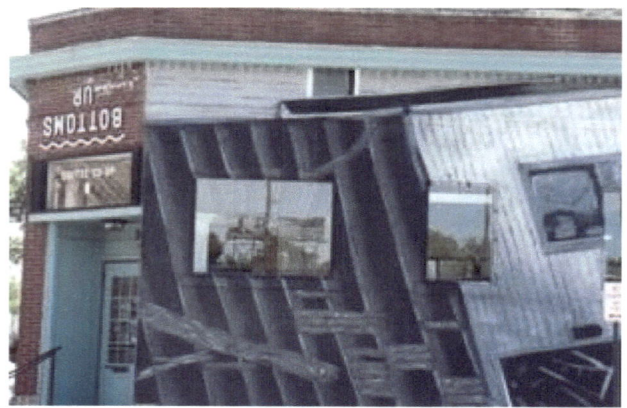
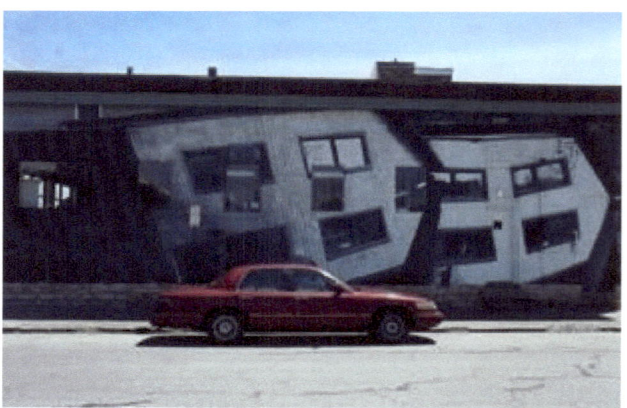
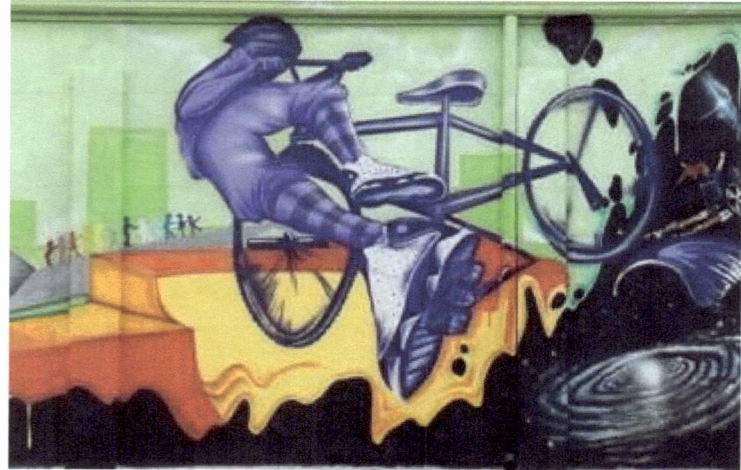
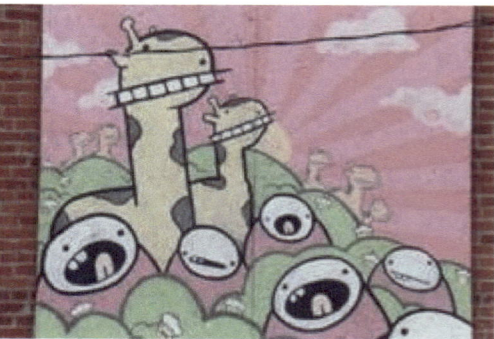

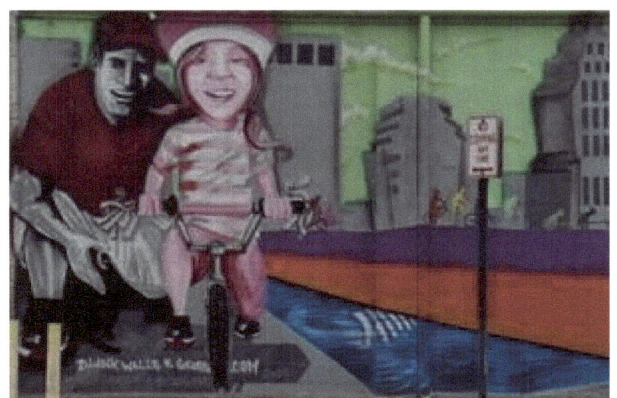
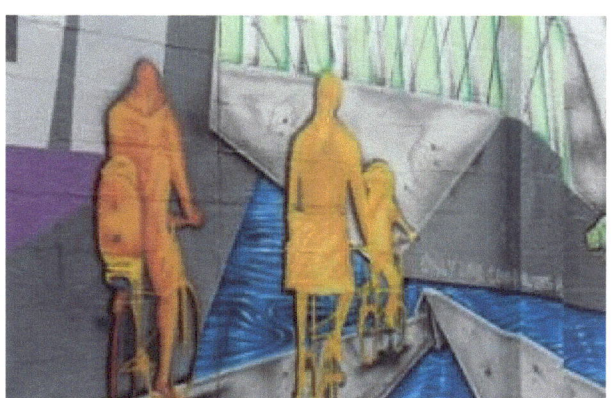
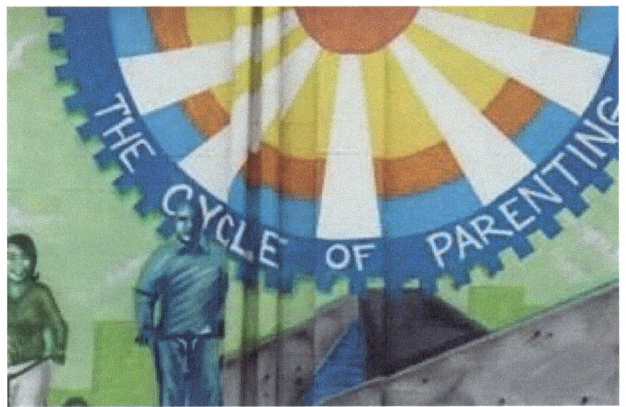
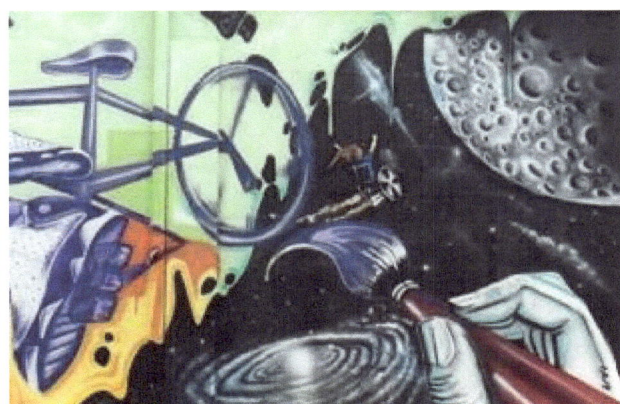
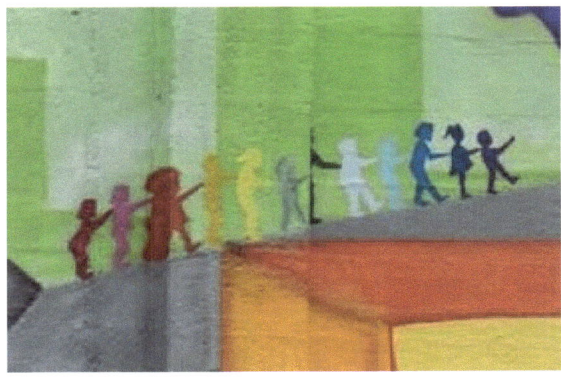

Murals and Street Arts in Franklinton Art District

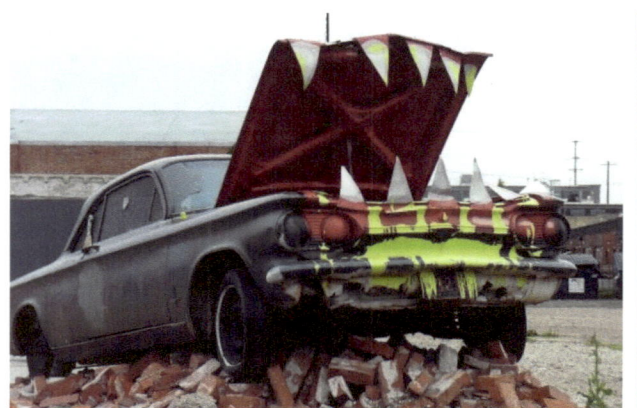 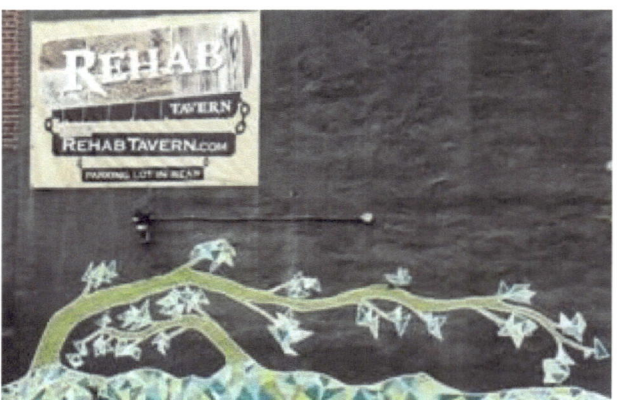

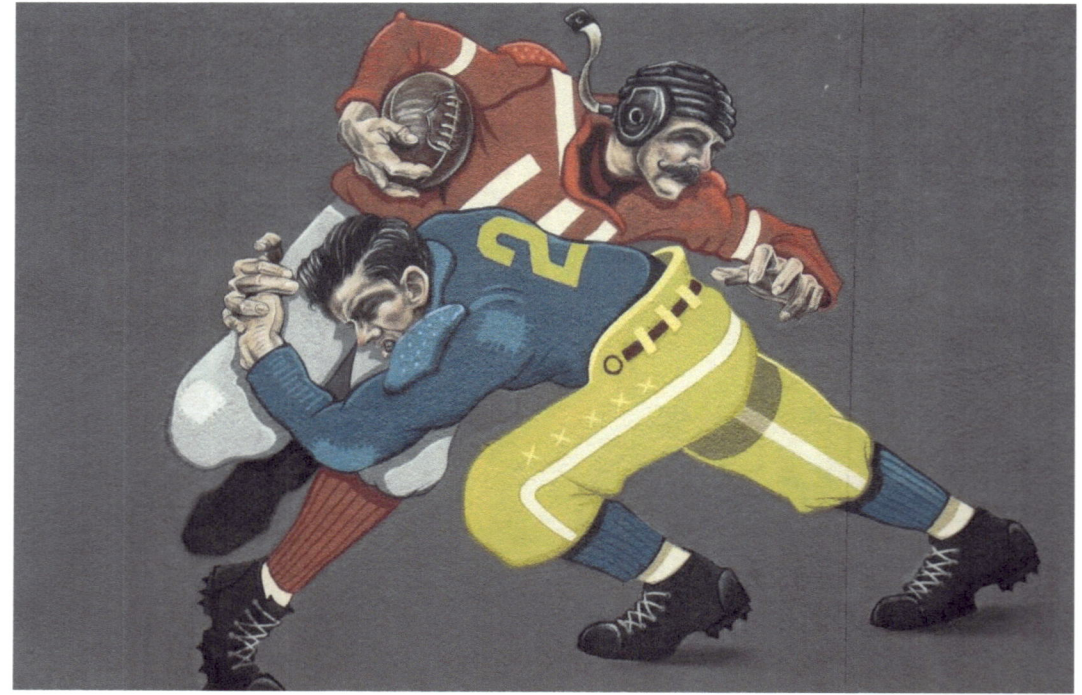

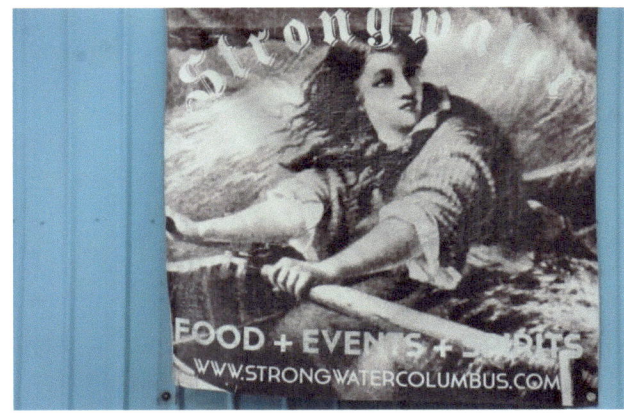

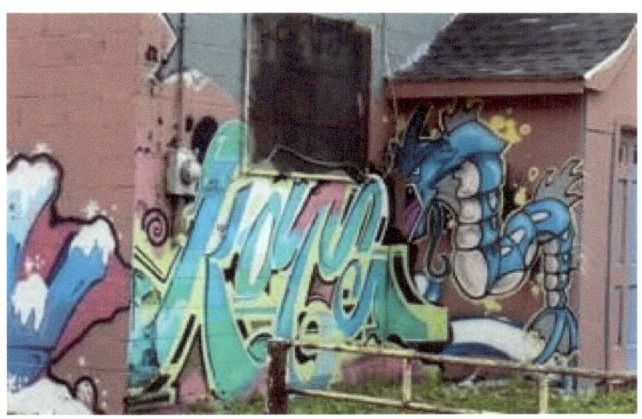

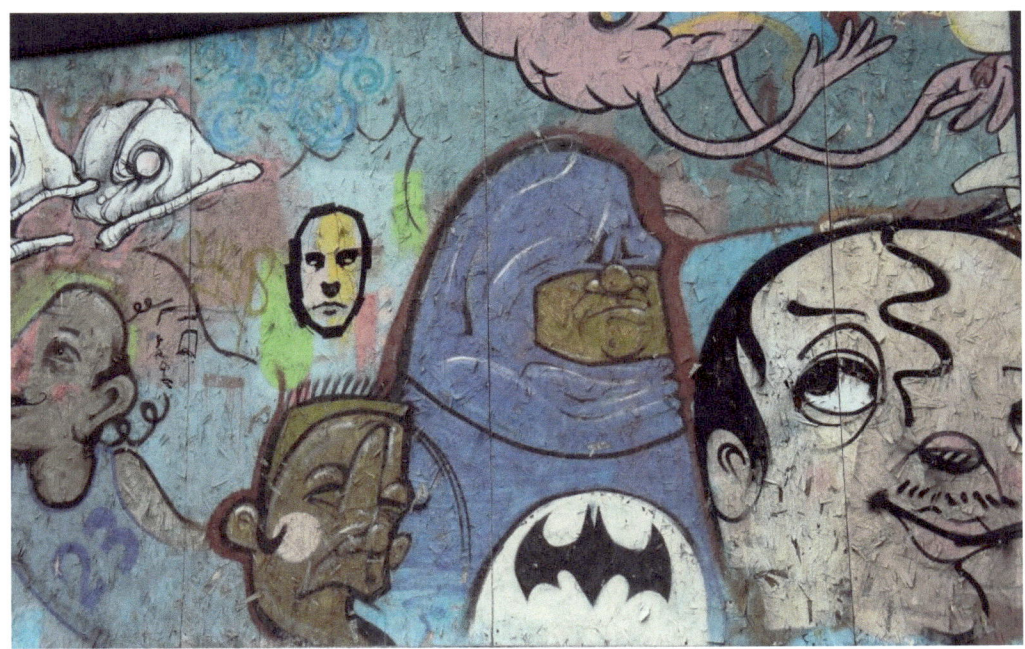

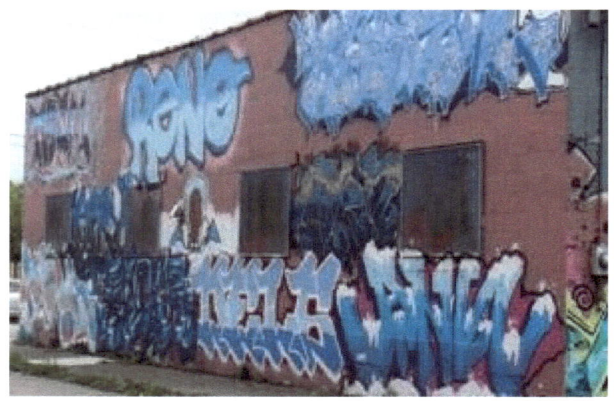
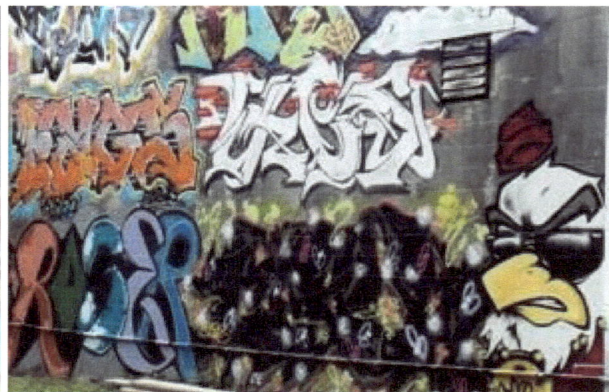
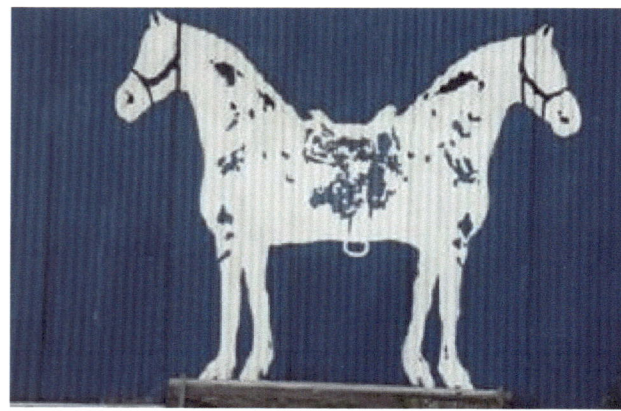
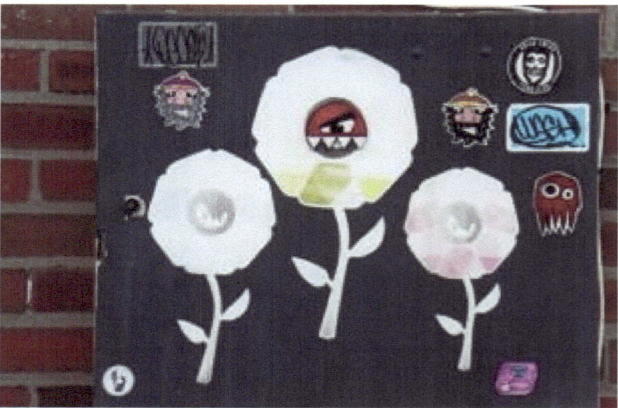

The Vanderelli Room at McDowell Street and W Rich St
Vanderelli Room Exterior

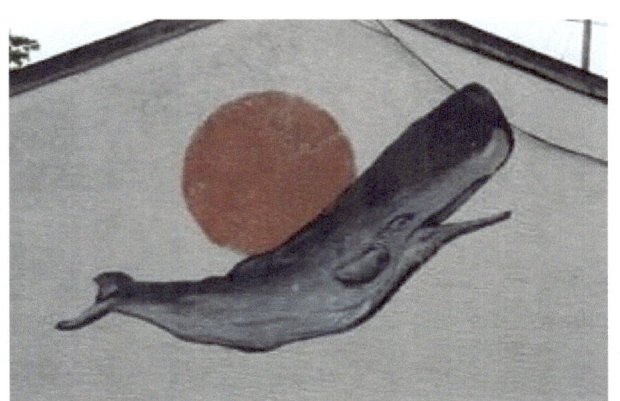

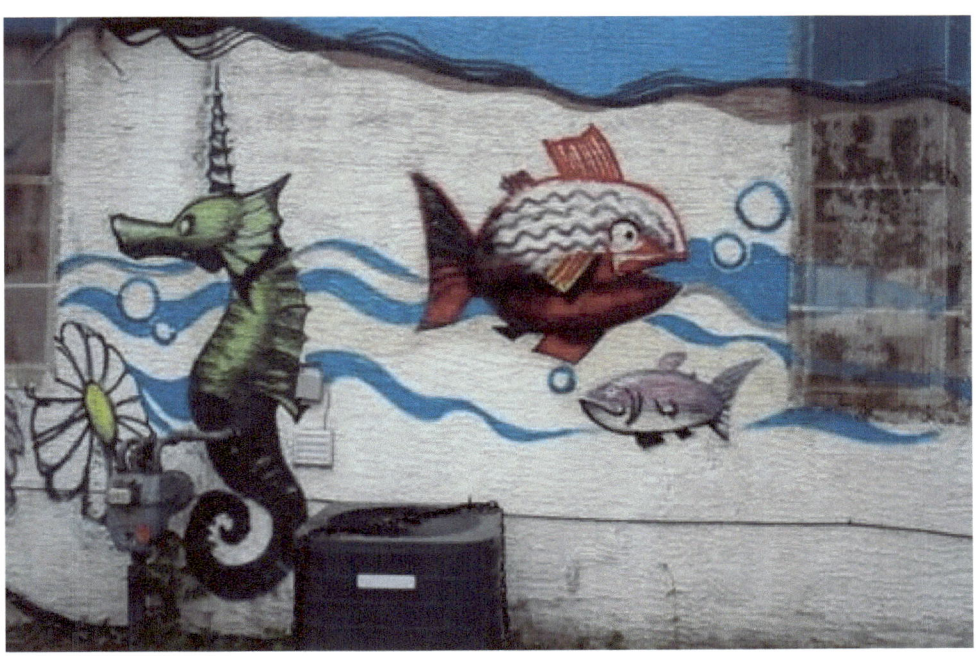

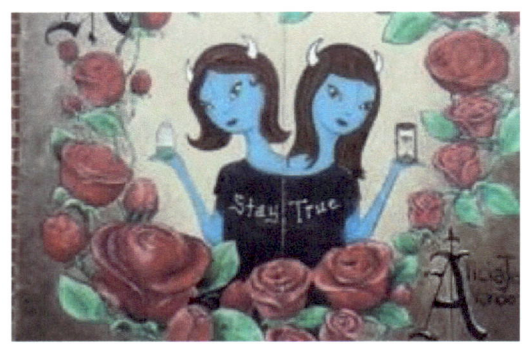
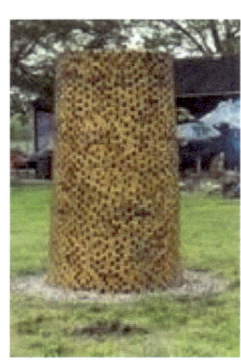
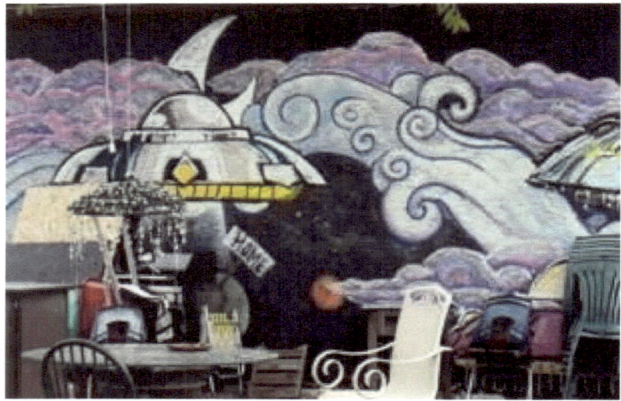
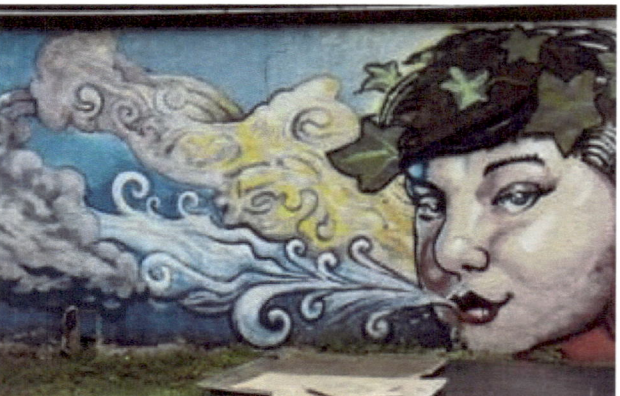
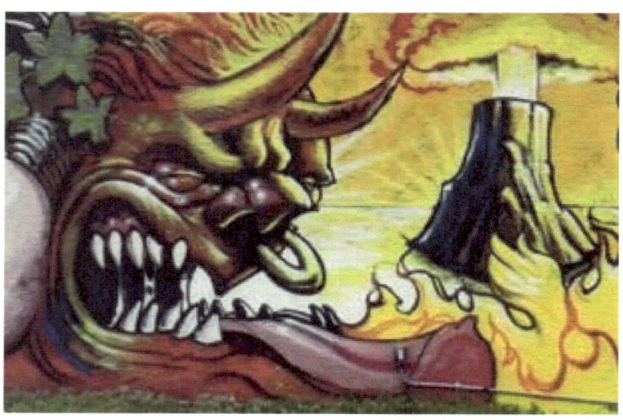
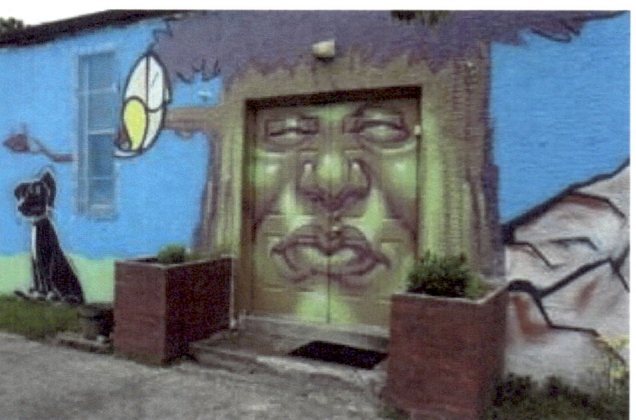

Arts displayed in the Vanderelli Room

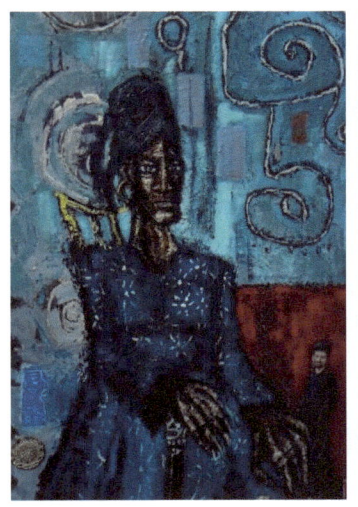 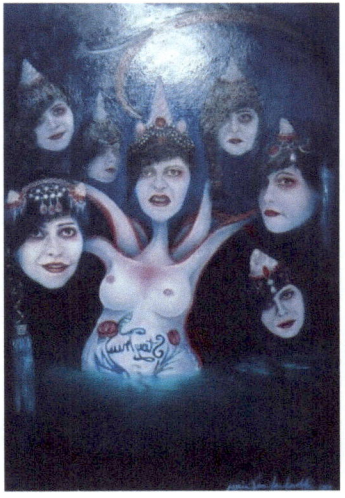 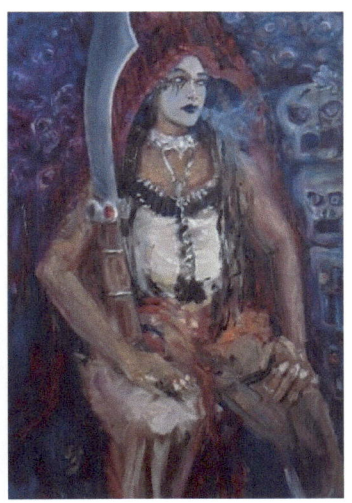

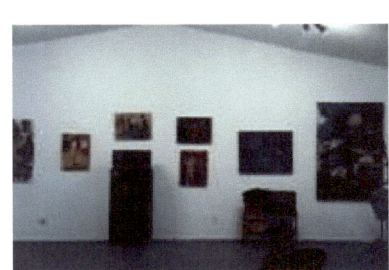 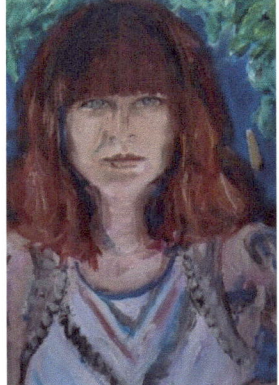 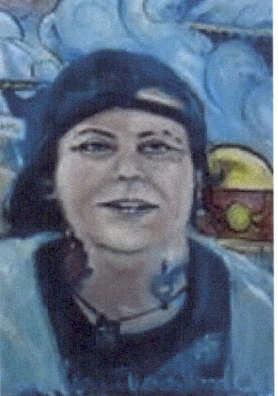 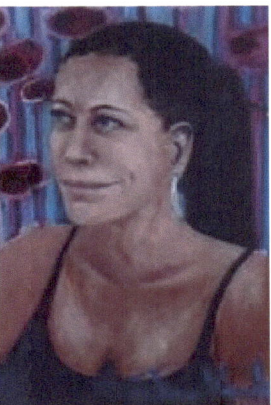

COSI at the east edge of Franklinton

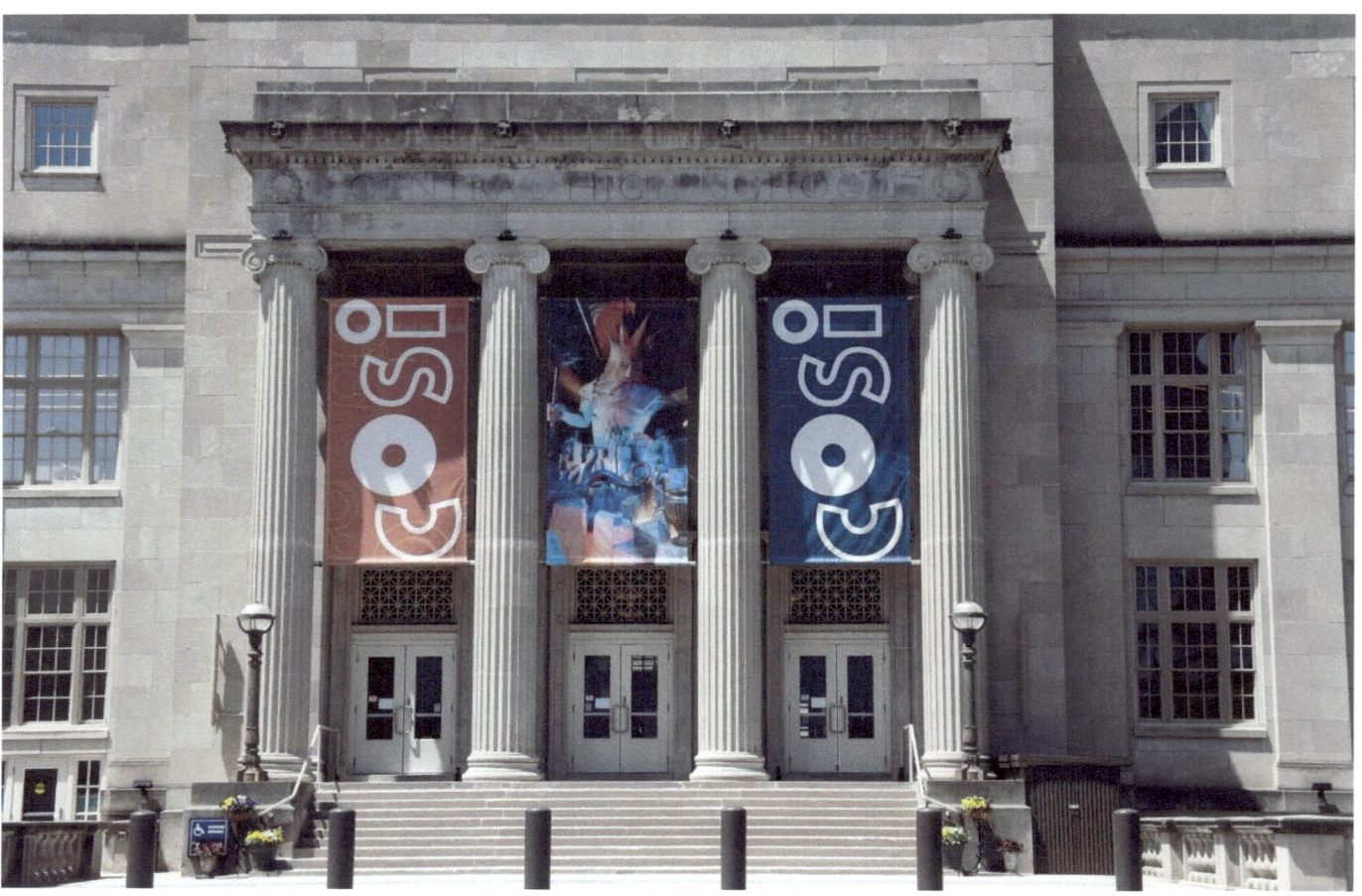

Veteran's Memorial Museum under construction in 2017 at the opposite side from COSI on W Broad St

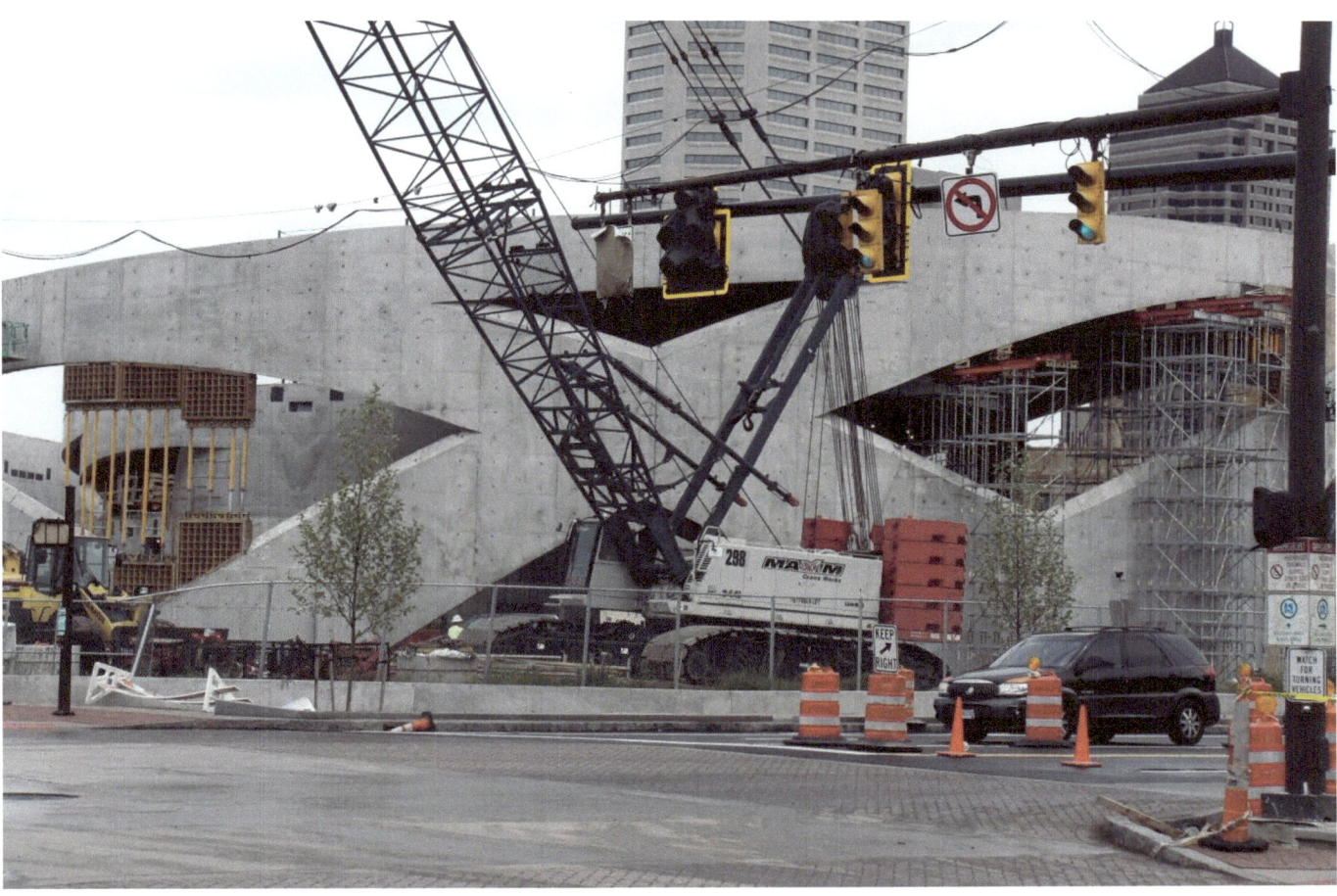

2017 Urban Scrawl Mural Auction Party

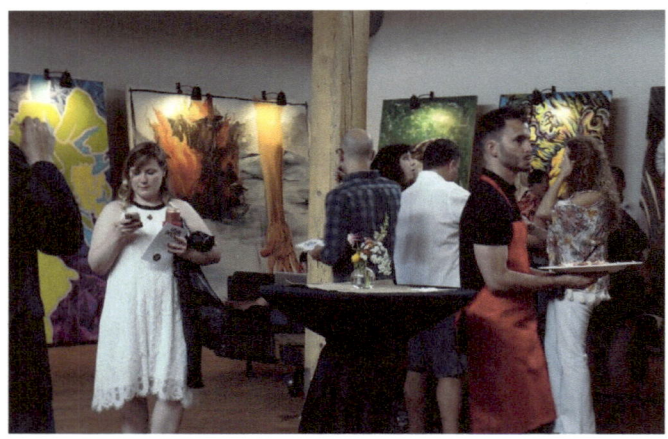

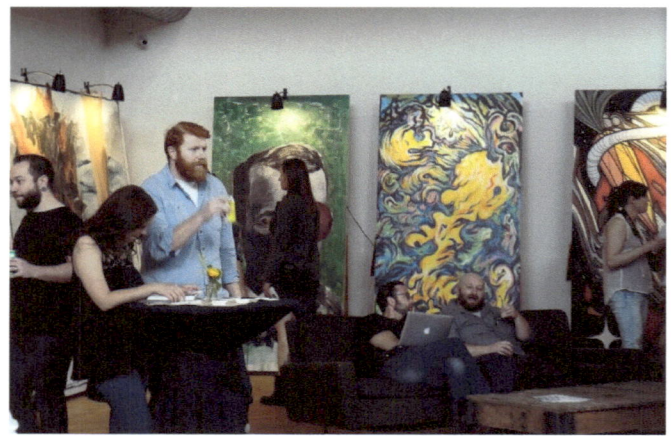

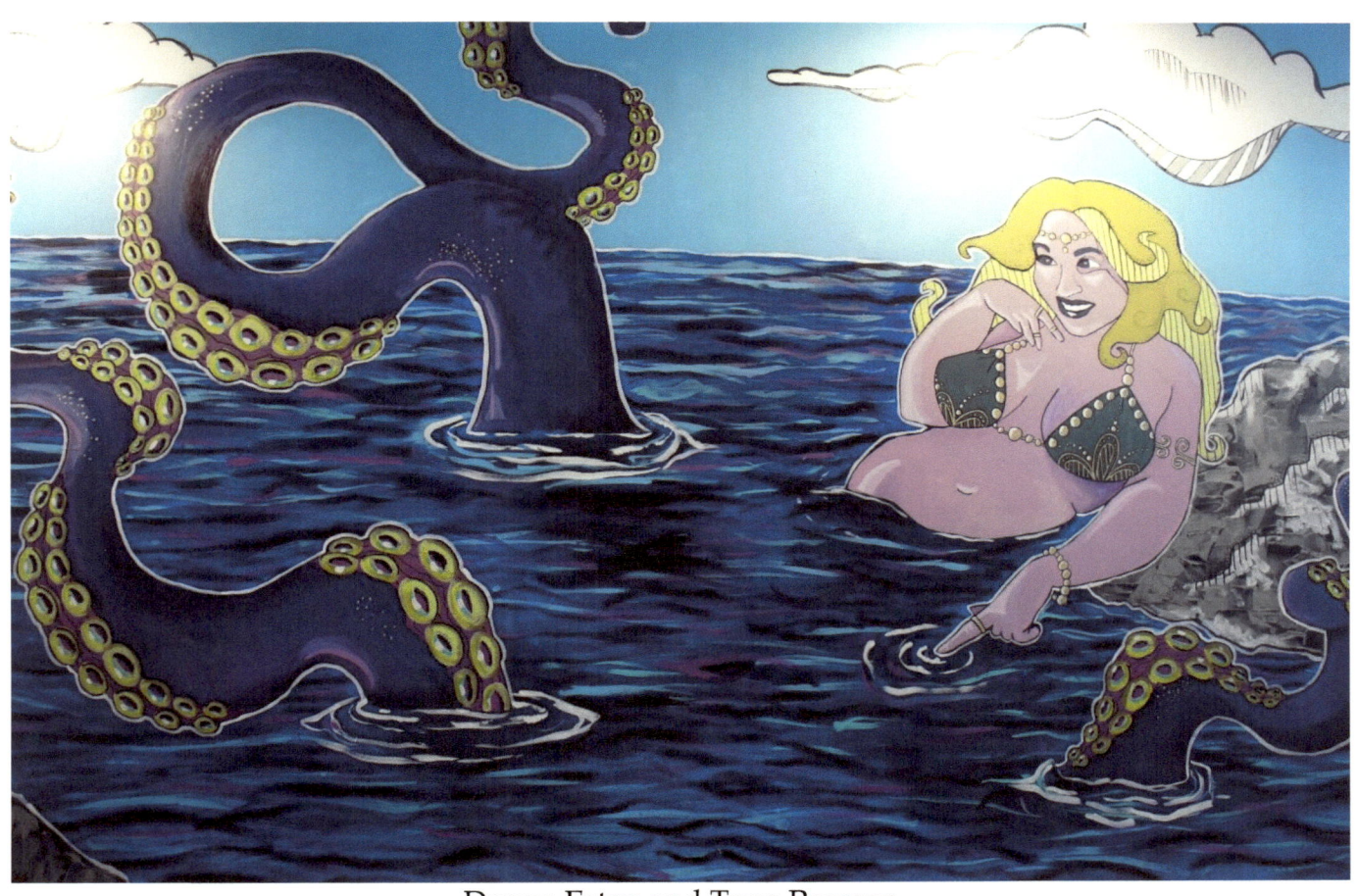

Donna Estep and Tona Pearson

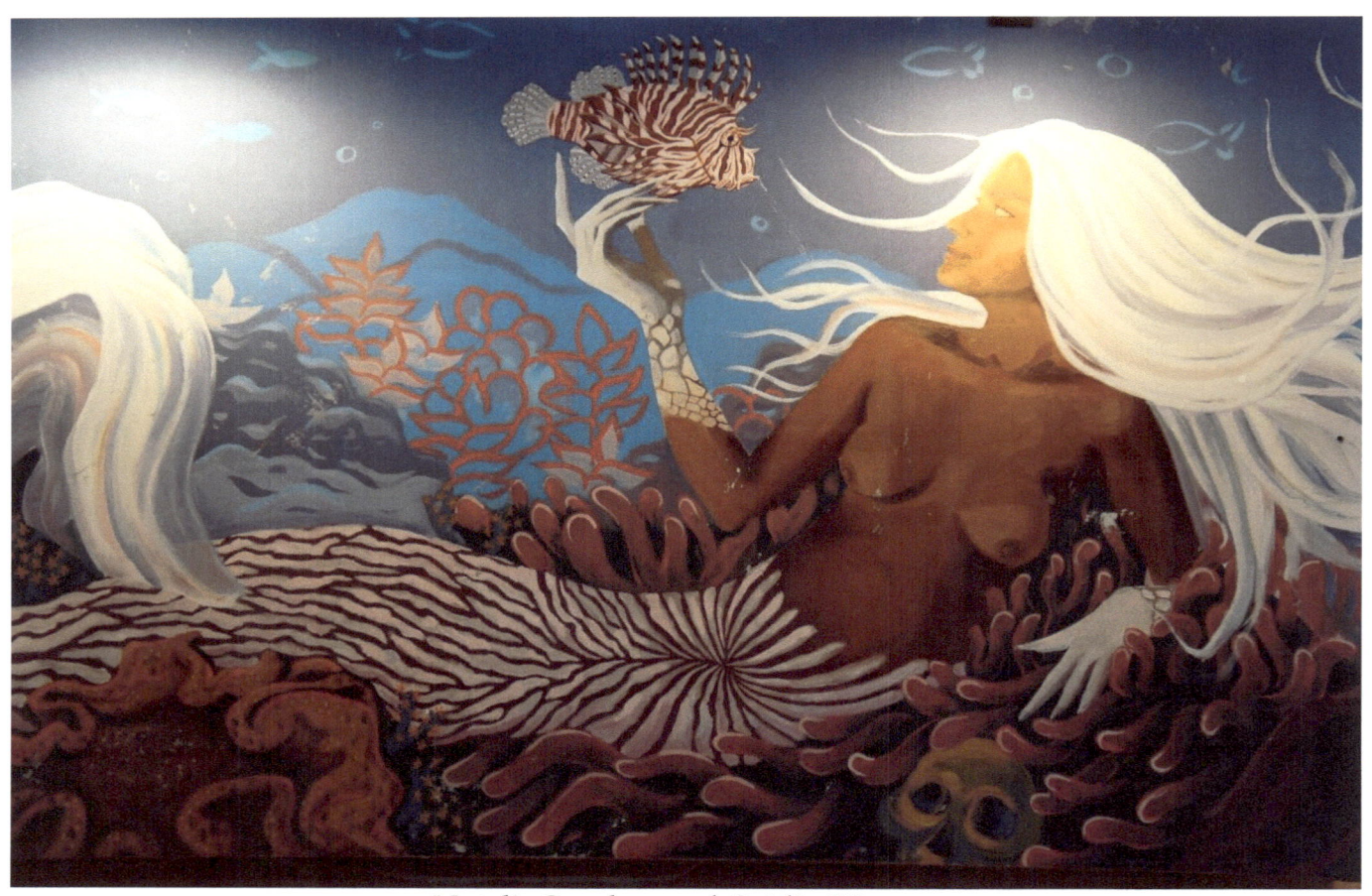

Natalie Sanchez and Caitlin Watters

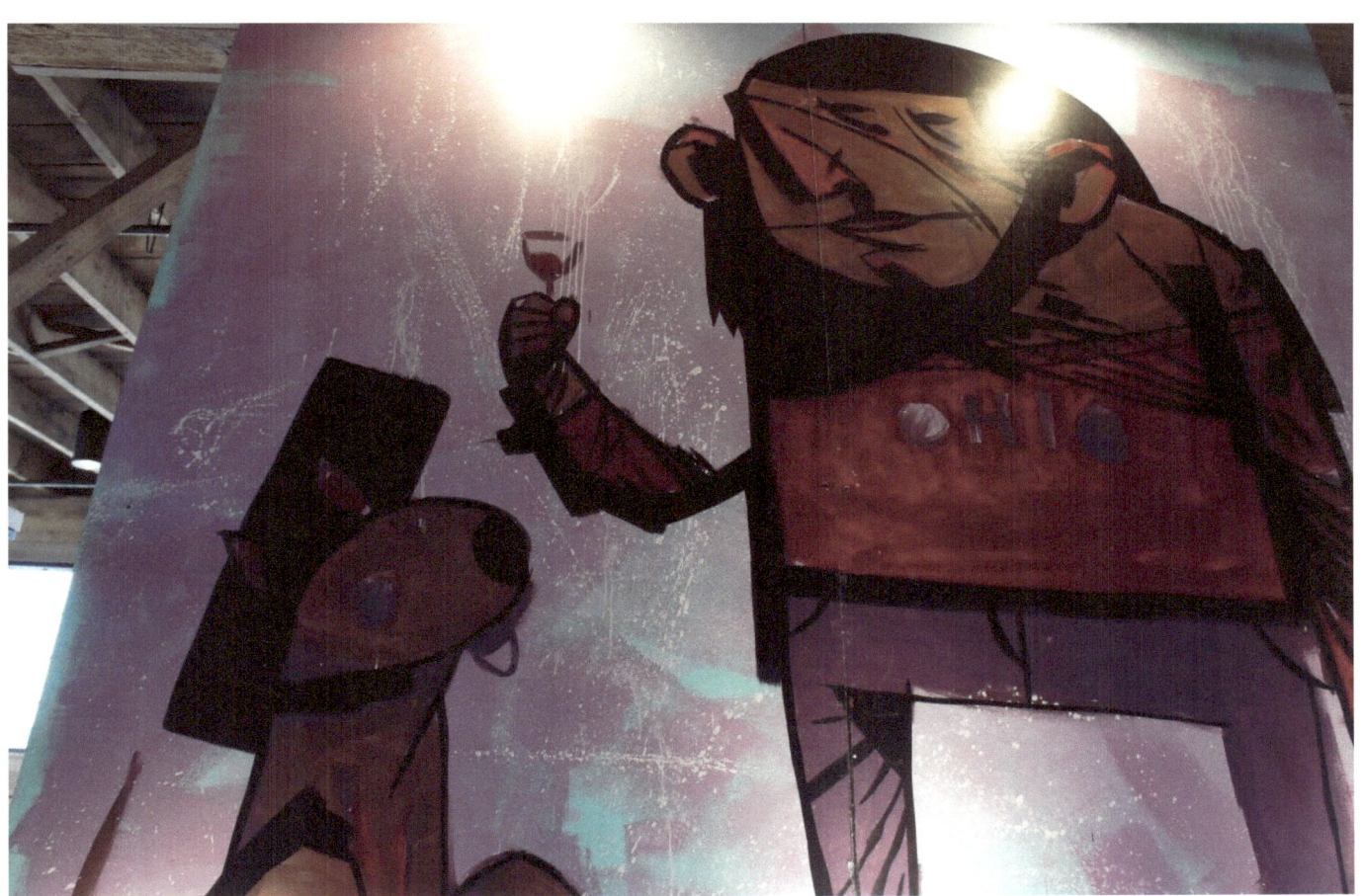

Thom Glick

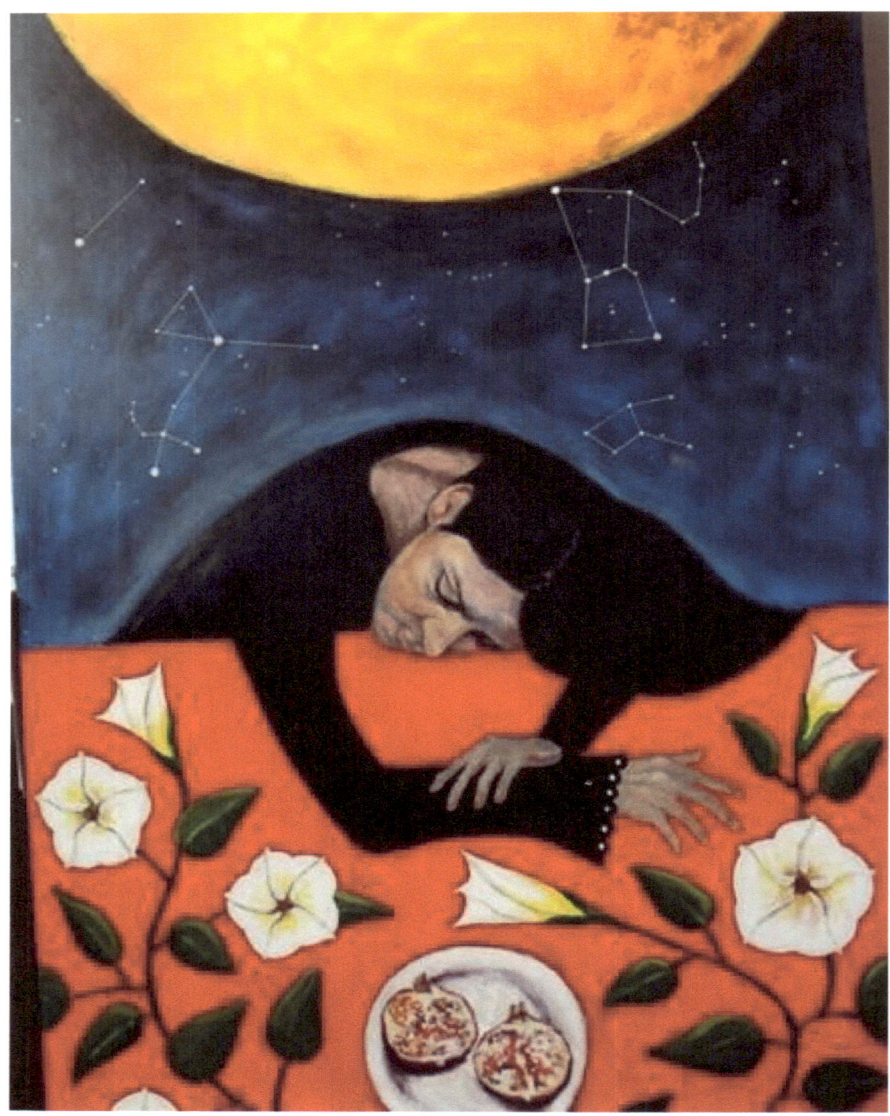

Hiroshi Hayakawa

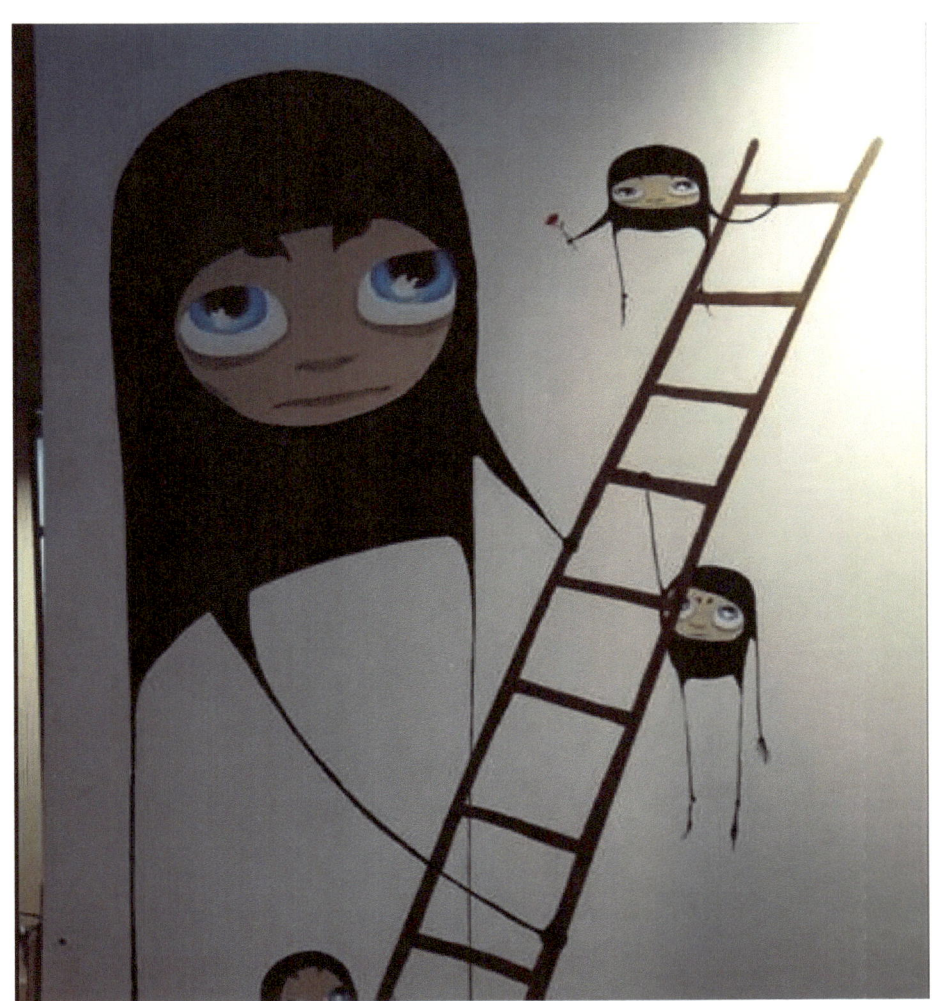

Mary Barczak

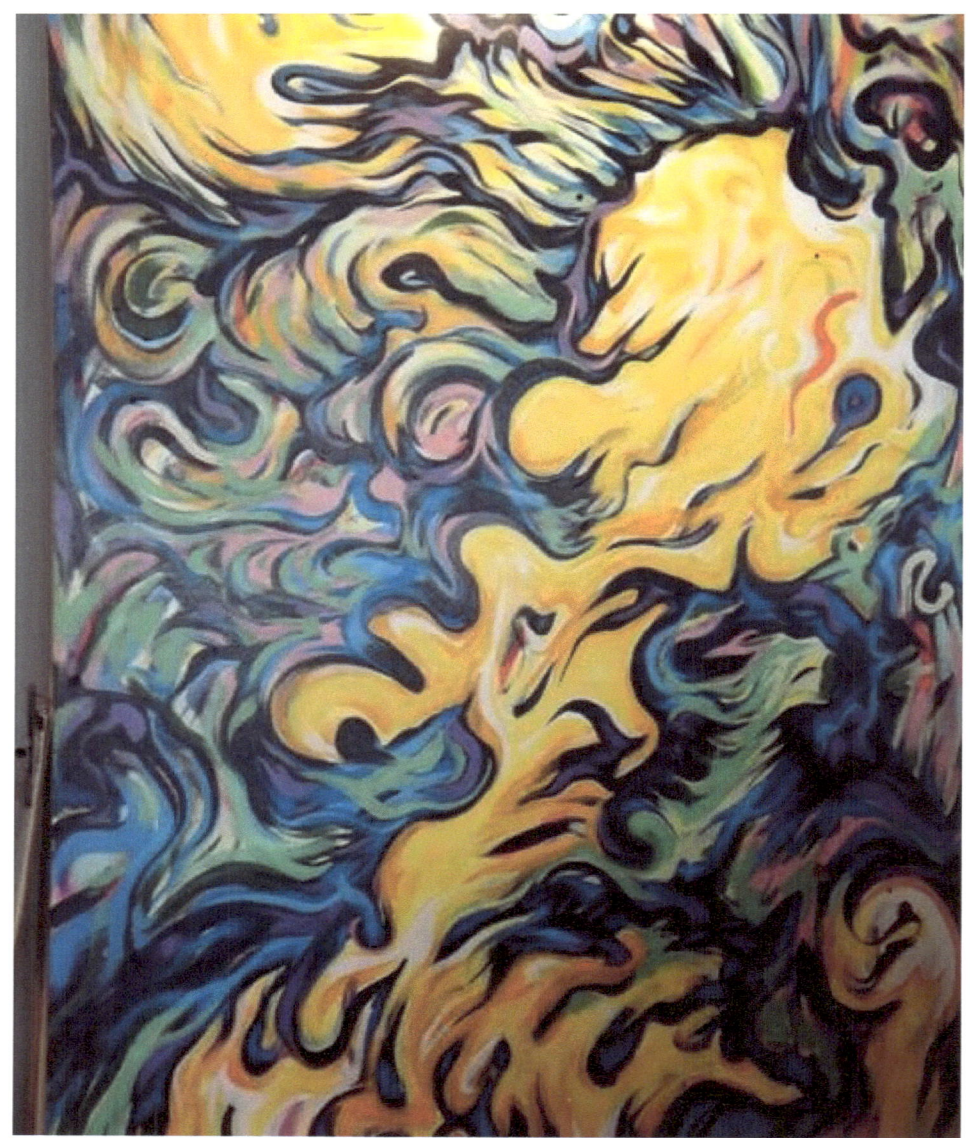

Jonathan Ryan

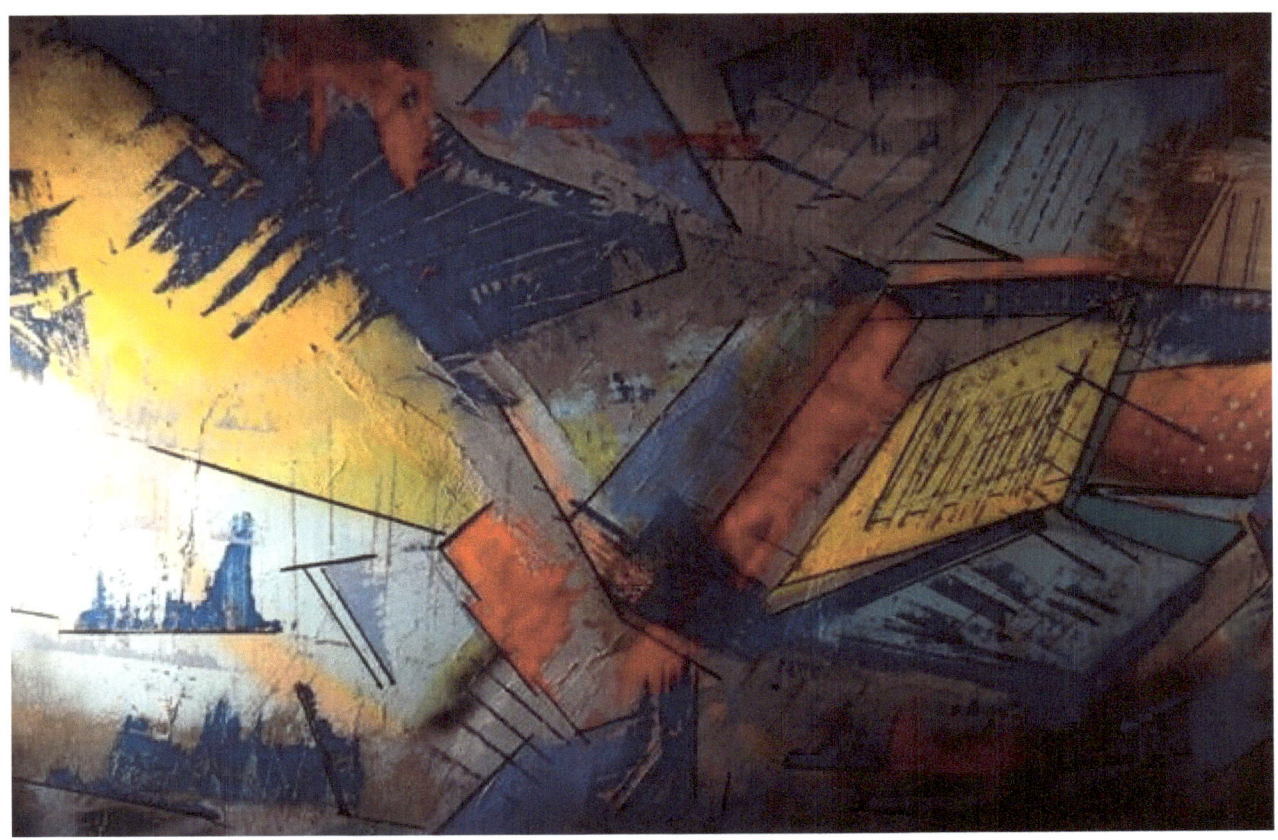

Cory Davidson

Glass Axis Gallery, 610 W Town St

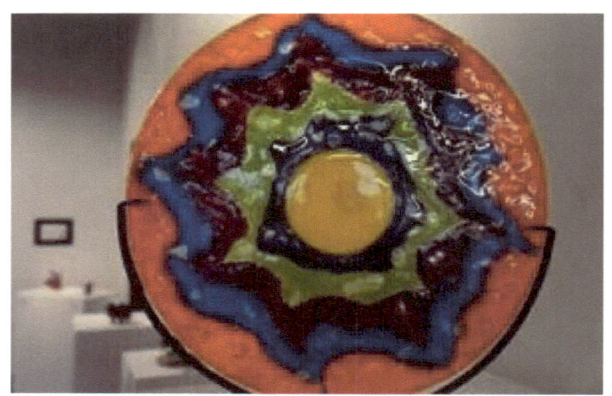
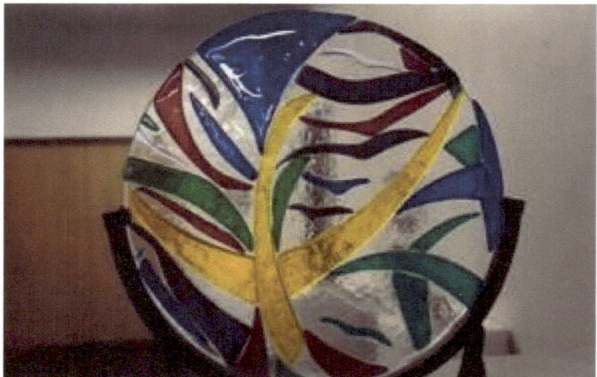
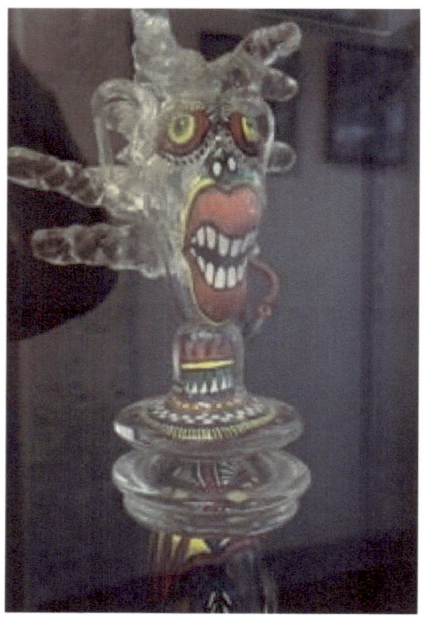
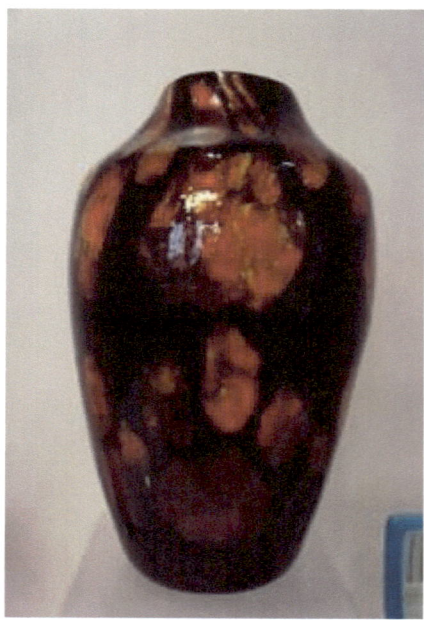

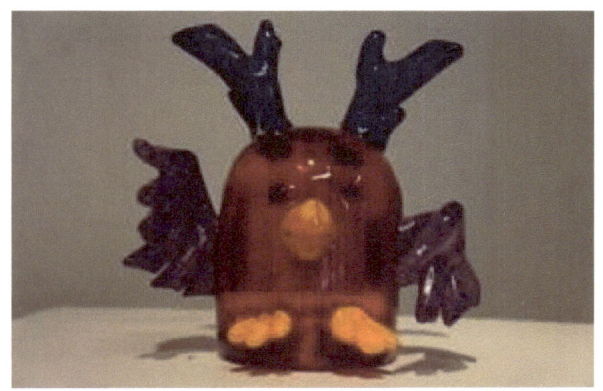
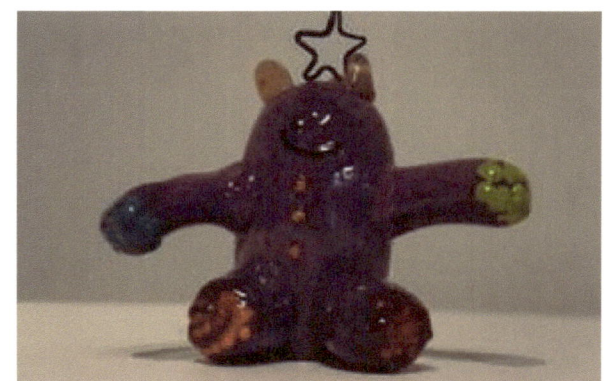
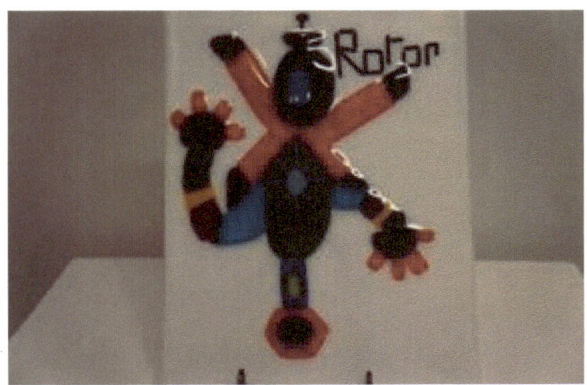
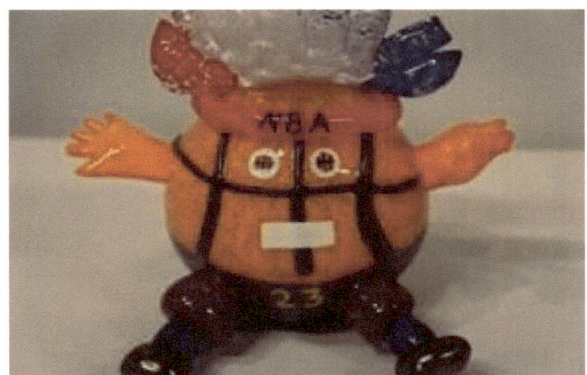
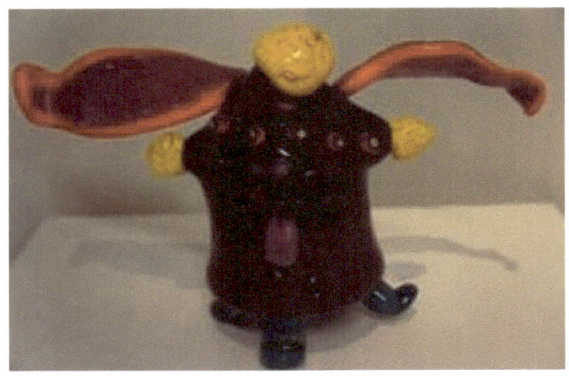
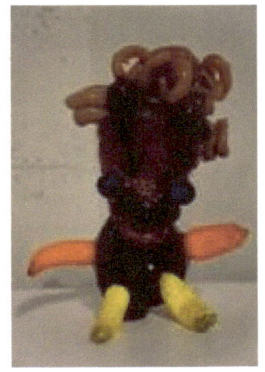
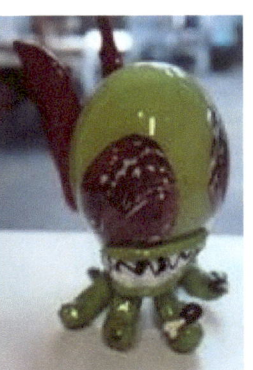

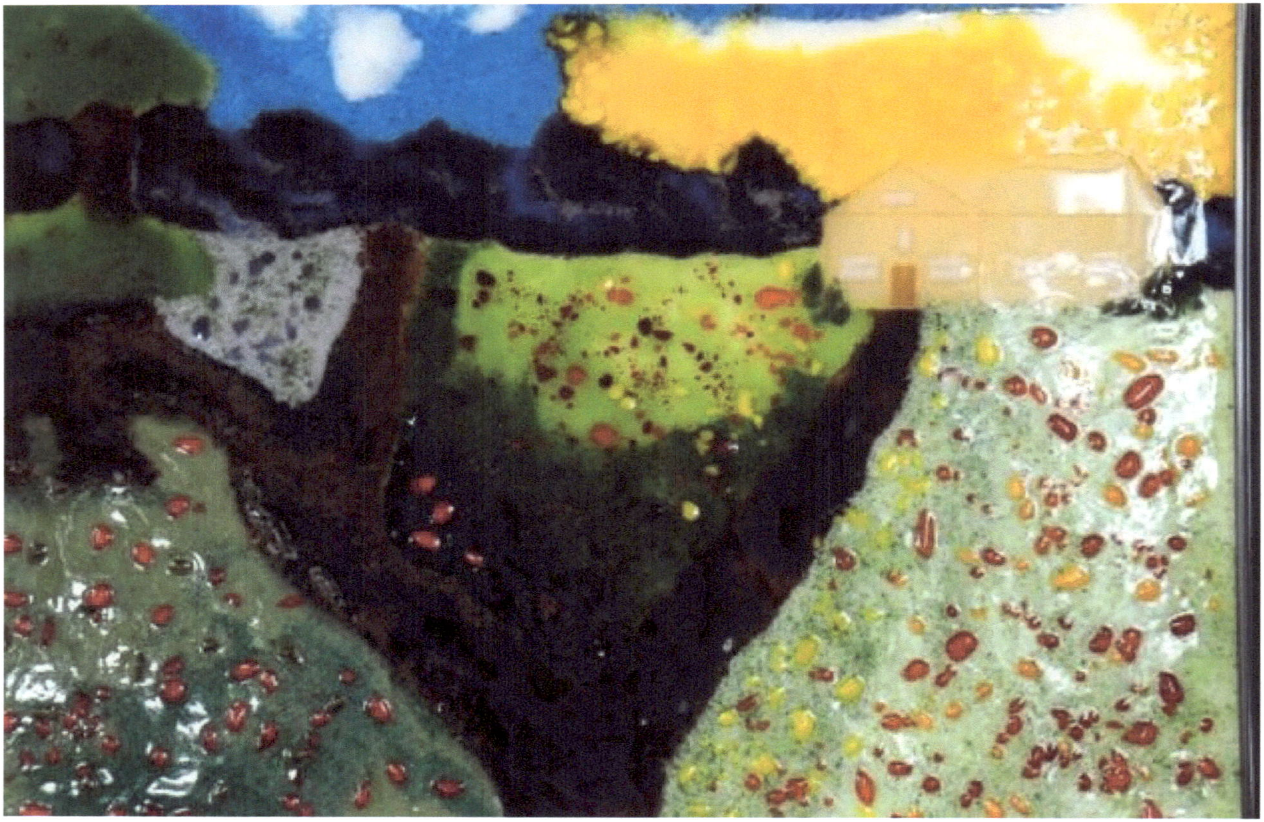

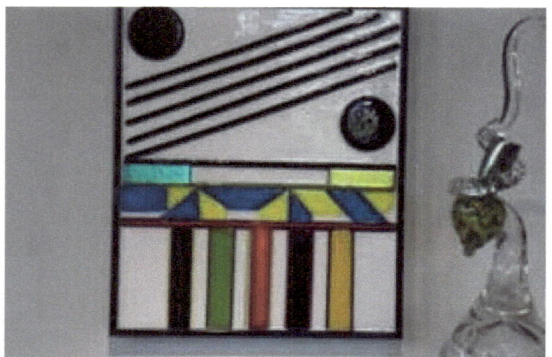

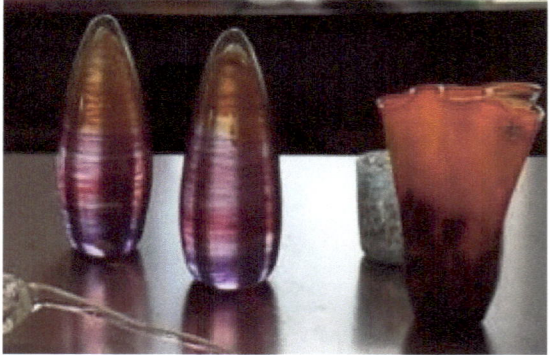

Art Market at 400 W Rich St. Opens every second Friday at 7PM

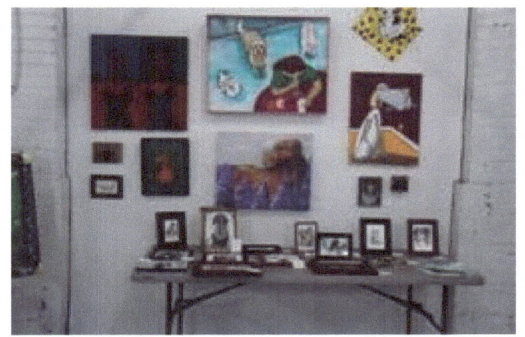 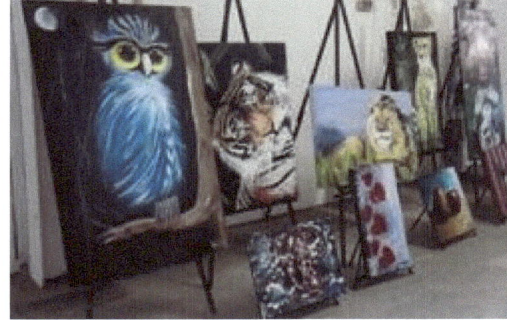

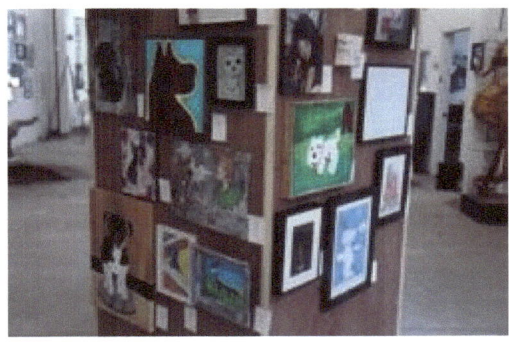 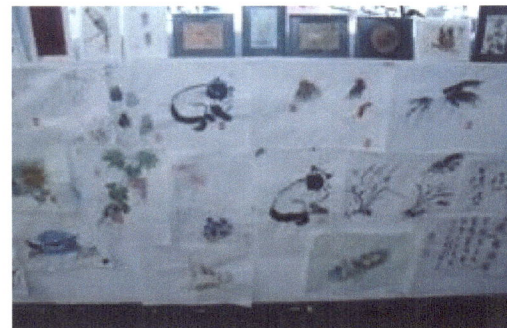

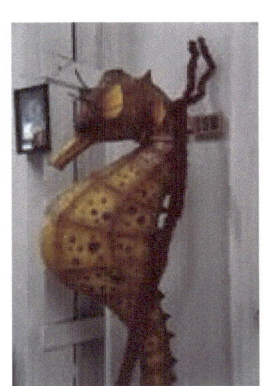 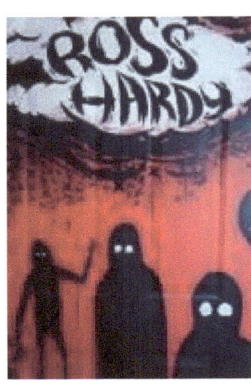 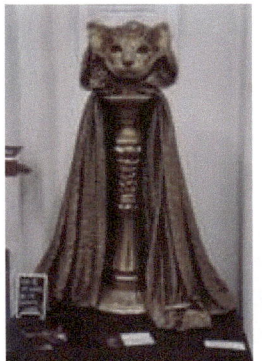 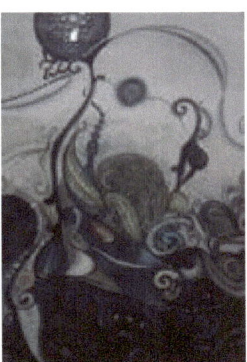

Cultural Arts in Columbus Book Series

Acknowledgements

The author expresses his appreciation to the assistance provided by Adam Herman for obtaining permission of including the photos of the Urban Scrawl Paintings and AJ Vanderelli in finishing this book. The author is also thankful to Rex Brown for his permission of citing in this book the photographs of the arts produced at Glass Axis.

www.ingramcontent.com/pod-product-compliance
Lightning Source LLC
Chambersburg PA
CBHW041302180526
45172CB00003B/931